HOPE IN DARK PLACES

Poems about Depression
and the Christian

— DAVID GRIEVE —

Sacristy
Press

Sacristy Press
PO Box 612, Durham, DH1 9HT

www.sacristy.co.uk

First published in 2017 by Sacristy Press, Durham

Sacristy Limited, registered in England & Wales, number 7565667

British Library Cataloguing-in-Publication Data
A catalogue record for the book is available from the British Library

ISBN 978-1-910519-67-7

To all with mental health illnesses

Foreword

Depression is both an experience that everyone has had—a passing lowering of mood—and also a common mental disorder (or illness). Simply speaking, depression is considered to be an illness when it lasts a long time, or becomes bad enough to interfere with everyday life. One in five people suffer from this kind of depression at some point in their lives. One in five people therefore know first hand what it's like to be depressed—and the rest of us will all know someone who has been depressed. Yet, depression remains widely misunderstood, not least amongst Christians.

A part of the problem is that we do all know what it's like to be low in mood. Much as we don't like such experiences, they usually pass. We therefore think that they should pass for other people too. But, what happens when they don't? It's all too easy to be unsympathetic, to imagine that we "know what it's like" or to offer trite solutions for "looking on the bright side". The reality is that we usually don't know what it's like—especially in the case of the more extreme forms that depression can take—and that simple solutions don't work. If they did, there wouldn't be a problem!

A complex conjunction of altered neurochemistry, adverse life events, altered patterns of thinking, and social alienation, the darkness of depression is rarely dispelled by the candles of well meaning words that optimistic people light. The torchlight of a patient, compassionate presence may have more impact on the darkness, but it's often easier to leave the darkened room than to turn on any lights, and so—as family and friends give up—the loneliness is increased, and the darkness deepens.

Sadly, Christians can be especially unsympathetic candle lighters, and Christians who are depressed can feel that their failure *as* Christians only adds to the darkness. Christians have "Good News" and, as every child in Sunday school knows, "Jesus is the answer"! If prayer has not made everything better and if, in the midst of the pit of depressive hopelessness, God seems not to care, then it is all too easy to lose faith. Guilt, anger, exhaustion, fear and anxiety eat away at all that is life giving, like a deadly and overpowering worm (see *Faith in Disorder*). In comparison with this, those who do not understand what they have not experienced easily, and unwittingly, only add to the hurt.

David Grieve knows that there are no simple remedies, and he knows just how tortuous the darkened corridors of depression can be. He has mapped them all in the ink of personal experience. He has struggled with the paradox of God's presence in the midst of experiences of God's absence and he knows that there is yet *Hope in Dark Places*, that "the presence you may not feel" is Christ's. As he writes in his Preface, these poems are "not about curing Depression, but about the companionship of Christ within it".

It is all too easy to tell people who are painfully aware of the absence of God that God really is with them, and in the process to be discouraging. David avoids the discouragement—and offers hope instead—at least partly, because it is so evident that he does not say this without a hard earned awareness of just how unbelievable it can seem to be. He avoids being simplistic or trite, also, because his faith is anchored in a deep awareness of the suffering, compassionate presence of Jesus, whose passion engaged with the full depth of human darkness. It is in this deeply Christian context that his understanding of what faith might look like in the midst of depression has been formed. As he writes in *That Deeper Darkness*:

The deeper darkness,
that smear you only just see out of the corner of your mind's eye as you contemplate ending it all,
that not-so-much-no-go area
as a darkness-he's-gone-further-into-than-anyone-else,

is where Christ is.

David has realised that honesty is hard won, and that being "real" is not achieved by jumping straight to a happy ending. Only by first speaking words that might appear to some as a loss of faith, is he able to plumb the depths of faith and find hope. As he writes in *Out of Darkness*:

I want you to be real; "victory" here is a lie.

It is deep down dark where God's blood meets mine;

only the dead God is any use to me.

Resurrection is pure moonshine.

But after the damage, Alleluias if he lives.

If he can, so may I break out of this hell

and sense again excitement and beauty.

Just never say I must always be well.

David has offered this book for people who, like him, suffer from depression. However, this is a book that all Christians should read. I say that not only because it will offer any Christian a deeper understanding of what it's like to suffer from depression, although that would not be a bad reason for buying this book. But, even more than this, it is a book about entering into the experiences of Jesus in Gethsemane and on Calvary. It is a book about being present with Christ in his suffering, just as it is about God's presence with us in the darkness of our suffering—whatever shape that darkness may take.

Chris Cook
Professor in the Department of Theology and Religion, Durham University
24 July 2017

Preface

These poems, which are not about curing Depression, but about the companionship of Christ within it, have been written over a thirty-year period, some during and some after illness or respite.

They are arranged in alphabetical title order and this seems to convey the changeability of my experience of Depression. I hope that they will be a resource that readers may dip in and out of whenever it is helpful.

I dedicate and offer them to all who, like me, are Depressives, whether or not they are currently ill, sometimes ill, or in remission.

Christ has blessed me in my many illnesses with his presence and the help of so many loved ones and health professionals, and I hope that this will be also the reader's experience.

I have been greatly helped in preparing this book by my publishers, and sincere thanks go to Richard Hilton, Thomas Ball, and all at Sacristy Press.

David Grieve
June 2017

Contents

Anagrams

When I am scared, O Lord,
you tell me I am sacred.
When I feel vile, O Lord,
you call me to live.
When faith is pale, O Lord,
you tell me to leap.
When trust saps, O Lord,
you remind me it will pass.
With you, O Lord, it is never too late.
That's the joy of the Gospel tale.

Candle

Light, quietly burning on wick in wax,
as my December struggles to defy the blackout
Be my Jesus

Light, quietly submerging,
as you drown in the wet of your own burning
Be my Jesus

Light, quietly put out,
as you lie discarded, useless, contradictory litter,
Be my Jesus

Comfort

I dare, as a Christian, to be depressed:
to make the heretic's admission of discontent,
of dis-ease and fear that will not relent,
I, who have drunk deeply of conversion's cup.

I know I go on about it
but I refuse to be falsely happy,
to connive, to be clappy,
when all the time life is hell.
I don't want to be cheered up,
prayed over, witnessed to, preached at, rebuked
like a deserter.

But I've looked
in the face of the triune God.
I've told him my grim tale
and, bless him, he kept his peace
and his eyes open. He sees
my grimness. That's a comfort.

Confirmation

Today I hear your voice
calling me,
choosing me,
confirming me as yours,
commanding me to serve,

my Father's voice, who made me,
my Saviour's voice, who came for me,
my Sanctifier's voice, who wells up within me.

So today I lift my voice,
loving you,
praising you,
entrusting myself to you,
confirming myself as yours

Today
    and tomorrow
        and always.

Every So Often it Must be Spoken Of

Taboo or not taboo.
That is the question.

People, for all sorts of reasons, take their own lives.
For some, it's the best, most honourable way.
Rather than be humiliated in battle they fall on their swords.
Or the loaded revolver or cup of hemlock is handed to them.
The impulsive self-killing for love's sake
carries a cachet of wept-for, vicarious romance
'brightening up' someone's screen.
Others drink or drug themselves in a fatal choice.

The breaking apart of the mind's ability to cope
when one straw becomes too many
is the last earthly act of a process,
though never the final word on their worth.

The man drawn to a cliff edge that entices and befriends
has a mind whose dense mass no one else can understand, in truth.
You have not been there, not where he is at that precise moment.
To empathise is not to know.

Anger, yours at him, yours at the reasons why,
is an emotion part-profane, part-holy.
The hush of the sotto voce gossiping
is drowned by the thunder from heaven,
a voice calling

> This, also, is my beloved child.
> There was no more that she could do.

Faith in Disorder

Do not fear, for I have redeemed you.
I have called you by name, you are mine

Just so.
This is my faith.
It is the song that my heart sends to my lips.
It is the wellspring of joy,
the fullness of hope.

But anxiety, the type that wastes your living like a worm crawling
through the gut, is a hidden, persistent predator.
Deadly and overpowering.

With the visible attacker, your scream comes early,
propelling you into fight or flight.

Adrenaline surges, and your body calls on unfamiliar strength.

The worm is sly, wearing you down,
eating you up before you know it
and attenuating you into surrender.

Those who have no time for this weakness because they have not
experienced it are not my attackers.

They may hurt me, but not as the worm does.

But when at last the worm has done its worst
blazing sunlight greets me,
so blinding that I may again have faith,
thankful for God's safe keeping.

February

These, for me (for M.E.),
the days when daylight begins to lengthen,
carefully measured like a train pulling out of a station,
gathering the power it needs to reach its destination,

are the pilot days,
the feeler days of the slowly stretching year
for health on probation,
days of trial and experimentation,
of waiting for the green shoots, the signs of restoration,
days of aching hope.

Feeling Better Again

Feeling better again doesn't mean I'm healed yet,
but I'm on the way.

Feeling better again is no guarantee I won't relapse,
but it's the shape of things to come.

Feeling better again gives no permission to try to get by on
my own, but does give me the power to try.

Feeling better again feels good.

God of Our Silent Tears

God of our silent tears,
There in the Garden,
Jesus our full heartache bears,
Weeps in submission.
In Pilate's house abused,
By Herod badly used,
God of our silent tears,
He suffered for us.

See how our flesh he wears,
By soldiers beaten.
Insults shouted in his ears,
Then execution.
In all his suffering,
He hung there as a King.
See how our flesh he wears,
He suffered for us.

God of our hopes and fears,
Defeating evil,
On the cross salvation nears,
His death kills evil.
He shouts our grief and loss,
He triumphs on the Cross,
God of our hopes and fears,
He suffered for us.

See how the curtain tears,
For "It is finished"
While he dies the darkness rears,
But death's abolished.
The Saviour lifted high
Means life and victory.
God of eternal love,
He conquered for us.

Head Lifter

PSALM 3

Head lifter,
you shattered the teeth of Depression
and rattled its bones in its skin.
It was your tablets which smashed its grip,
you who made darkness friendly
and gave mystery meaning
and frustrated the fear.

The helpers were many.
The credits are endless.
But deliverance belongs to the Lord.

Hope in Dark Places

He has been there,
and the presence
you may not feel is his.
As you reach out blindly
he sees as you cannot,
and he prays.

The fellowship of the
completely alone
centres on him.
There is no length
to which he will not go
to keep you safe.

You need do nothing
because that is what you can do
until, as you begin to believe
that the first gleam of light is real,
the ability to be recovered,
buried in dark earth for so long,
shoots and grows in the unfamiliar
air of new hope.

Paralysis will be converted to stillness
in the same Way as his hanging
silenced the powers of darkness
and caused the tombs to erupt and empty.

How To Be, Depressed.

Being depressed is the simple part.
The spiral starts and I am helpless.
Each night, each morning,
gets progressively worse.
Any buoyancy worked up
at 11pm is cruelly gone by 3am.

But how to be? How to exist?
There is no ability to cope.
Appetite vanishes. Thewallsclosein.
There is little to do and so much time
to do it in.

A Sudoku puzzle, maybe, maybe not.
Laying the fire, 5 minutes.
I hoover a square of carpet
and am exhausted.

I flee from the phone,
from the doorbell.
Going to church is out of the question.
If God wants me, he'll have to come and get me.
Kind words wash over my head.
I tend, through experience, to blot out
well meant absurdities.
I cannot write, or read, or think.
The mind is dead.

There comes a point
when I don't want to be.
Here or anywhere.
I've never attempted,
but self-harm and suicide
become friends who understand,
who offer compassion, the only hope.

When I begin to notice
that I'm still here,
and that what drugs
can offer begins to happen,
I allow a chink of hope. Only a chink.
But recovery has got a foot in the door.
I can't be sure that I won't get well.

I Fear, It's Jesus

Come in through the padlocked door,
be the antidote to fear.
Let your presence chase it out,
gate crashing, resurrected Lord!.

Come into the hopelessness,
the Mary, Martha grief-struck fear.
Let your weeping chase it out,
o'ercoming, overriding Lord!.

Come into the sinking Church,
be the antidote to fear.
Let your speaking chase it out,
commanding, awe-inspiring Lord!.

Living Free

I bite back (when I've got my teeth in),
and the black dog howls and whimpers
and slinks away, a cringing cur.

The pain of countless savagings,
when the dog was a wild-eyed monster,
has subsided. Drugs put a buffer zone of safety
around the hunted mind.

The peace is exhilarating,
and liberates me into the sheer joy
of everyday life. I can laugh at winter
when there is no ice in the soul,
when the mind is not paralysed
by the grim grip that will not let go.

Naturally, there are laws to obey
in the land of the unpursued.
Be vigilant. Be kind to the tamed,
not vengeful, but wary of the wild.
Keep your hands well away from his jaws,
and don't goad the caged beast.

Look over your shoulder but not in fear.
Let your gaze roam and senses feast
on the granted fruits. You are not
Tantalus; they will not be snatched away.

And should you ever need him,
the Keeper is near at hand.

Marbles

We lost our marbles, the cat and I.
They rolled under the sofa while we played.
We know they are there, but we cannot get them back.
God is good at shifting furniture.

May I Stress?

Can I have your at_tension, please?
Listen to my growing.
Even though I'm a groan man, I must complain.
Even though the outcome is God, the infeel is pain.

They crabbed me in the back, and I am fished out, gutted.
I fillet in my bones.

Sense?
Rather, feeling.

The puzzle is being down, and the solution is a cross_word.

For God blurted, committed, came.
And it will be all_right.

Moments of Clarity

I might wish to be speaking of some titanic moment
upon a wine-dark sea,
or looking out across a vast azure horizon
that all the ages have longed to cross
and none have been able but me.

I might wish to tell of disclosure granted to no one else,
the drawing back of a curtain in sacred space
that only I witnessed,
and no one else was able to see.

But it's never like that. God's mysteries are plural,
shared in the congregation,
the collection of differently operating minds which comprise a unity,
formed in reaction to revealed grace.

There have, I suppose, been a few moments of clarity
over the years at times of exhaustion, rather than exhilaration,
not the easy, care-less times, never the luxury of untested trust,
but the first prayer after the well has run dry,
when I say God will provide, and I mean it.

Not Now But Later

In winter soil shifts,
rain-washed,
hoof-hammered,
mole-turned,
and not always un-manned.

In winter
no foliage fronts fear,
no energy eases ennui,
no colour camouflages callous,
aching grief.

In winter
the very deadness
shreds itself into
nature's kind anaesthesia,

Unimaginable resurgence ahead.

Old Testament Lesson

PSALM 13

David's deep and depressed,
forgotten, rejected, oppressed,

Dejected anointed king
left lonely and suffering

Blames God for hiding his face
(how long till he gives his grace?)

But finds his fears and cries
his own worst enemies

Repented anointed king
recovers the power to sing.

On Reading Philip Larkin on Death's Approach in Old Age

Smiles are for youth. For old age come
Death's terror and delirium.

Is it better, braver, nobler
to have no near grave comfort?
Is it fact facing and honest
and in the circumstances the only attitude to have,
since God,
to look forward just to decay
and the dispersal of the elements which comprised me,
and so grim and bear it?

Or did age misread the script youth sent,
and is it braver to eschew that virtuous gloom
and fall back on the fun of faith,
looking for joy in the mourning?

One of These Days

One of these days
will be the new day.
I will not be enraged.
One sock will not have vanished
in the bowels of the washing machine.
Pets will be continent,
children tidy,
machinery reliable,
governments good.
Poets will not use words only they have heard of.
Death by a thousand distractions will be a thing of the past.
I shall be satisfied, one of these days.

Out of Darkness

Long since I came out as Depressive;
surprising myself if not others, I named it,
gave it a shape, a shade, called a spade a spade.
I held up the pill bottle to the light.

That was before the even darker nights,
the smothering of carrying on as if normal,
the death of life and then the life of death
and so sheer bloody awful.

Each illness stops when it runs out of darkness,
surrendering at last to persistent light
that heals and restores and gives permission to live
until the next slide into the grip of night.

Ach! Don't you ever platitude to me,
do not dare to try to cheer me out;
all you can do is bear some of my weight
and stop me crying the final shout.

I want you to be real; "victory" here is a lie.
It is deep down dark where God's blood meets mine;
only the dead God is any use to me.
Resurrection is pure moonshine.

But after the damage, Alleluias if he lives.
If he can, so may I break out of this hell
and sense again excitement and beauty.
Just never say I must always be well.

Reaching Out

I will not accept that
restoration means going back to where I was.
I will not accept
that the well is forever dry, nor lost the cause.
    But I'm reaching out towards the unknown,
    The imprecise, the as yet ungrown.

I listen to your words
of sincerely, lovingly meant re-assurance.
I listen to the songs
of comforting Christian assurance.
    But I'm reaching out towards the unknown,
    The imprecise, the as yet ungrown.

I abide by the codes of
inherited, time-proved behaviour.
I abide in the love of
an exalted and personal Saviour.
    But I'm reaching out towards the unknown,
    The imprecise, the as yet ungrown.

So Well, So Much

He knows us so well; he loves us so much.
He does not ignore or pretend not to know
    the darkness surrounding,
    the weakness impeding.
He knows us so well; he loves us so much.

He loves us so much; he counted the cost.
He did not recoil or pull back from our flesh;
    He embraced our humanity,
    He shouldered our poverty.
He loves us so much; he counted the cost.

He counted the cost; he submitted to shame.
He freely and humbly accepted our loss,
    the darkness absorbing,
    the weakness transforming.
He submitted to shame; he loves us so much.

Saying It Again

REFLECTIONS ON FENWICK LAWSON'S
PIETA IN DURHAM CATHEDRAL

Saying it, as at the beginning,
now at the ending,
at the foot of the cross,
he, taken down lifeless Son of God,
her son,
first born, child of such promise. Contorted

He lies there,
all breath extracted
and hardly a breath in her,
rooted in the rock hardness of grief.

Dropped hands are open,
unclenched,
in the *let it be* position
of helpless love's letting go.

Eyes numbed shut,
she does not see how,
in rigor mortis,
a distended arm sticks up as if
to grasp her by the hand.

It is too early for her to believe
but soon he will overturn
such relentless certainty
and invite her into the
let it be
of resurrection.

The Bush is Still Burning

EXODUS 3

That moment of exhaustion,
of having nothing new, nothing fresh,
nothing left to pray
is breakthrough.

The resigning from having to talk at God,
to tell him the news,
to sum up the world's crises
in ever such a neat liturgical framework,
the agitation of being empty and spent and over

is where self begins to end and
prayer ends its beginning.

The angel appears.
The ground is holy.
The bush is still burning.

That Deeper Darkness

Birthed in an up-alleyway-café,
amid generous, kind, laughing, over-spilling hospitality,

Who'd have known, imagined, suggested,
that this poem could actually have been conceived
in that deeper darkness, that winter-never-ending blackness,
that Christmas-crushing, hope-smashing inner utter awfulness
that the un-ill-with-it may never realise needs to be named,
owned, capitalised, there-I've-said-it Depression.

The light at the end of the tunnel
(so say all of us Depressives only a quarter joking)
is the train coming to smash you.

The deeper darkness,
that smear you only just see out of the corner of your mind's eye as
you contemplate ending it all,
that not-so-much-no-go area
as a darkness-he's-gone-further-into-than-anyone-else,

is where Christ is.

Therapy

We sat,
eight of us,
in the too familiar room
and the woman sobbed and shook.

There were also eight ribs
either side of the central spar
of the radiator,
and the vinyl chairs shone blackly.

She sobbed,
and we waited,
shifted,
scratched
and kept the rules.

The therapists maintained
their professional stillness,
give nothing away eyes
targeting the floor.
Occasionally
I looked at the glass wall,
my way of showing the observers
that I'm a professional too,
and I'm not intimidated.

I counted the minutes
off the clock on the wall.
Each prickly ninety minutes
was a lake of silence
littered with abandoned bridges
that never quite made it across.

The woman was blowing her nose.
The therapists asked whether
it was fear
or just distress she felt.

She said 'I need a friend'.
They said 'It's time to end'.

When I Write I Live

Oh, I am stymied!
The writer says: Depressed?
Then write, be healed.
But, depressed, I cannot write.
I cannot hear the music,
listen out for the rhythm.
There is silence, nothing revealed.

Sure, the horrendous squeeze
of the deep dark pressurises:
there is hidden pearl-making
by the irritation of the grit.
It spills out later, but is made then, I realise.

Poetry makes me live.
I agree with her here: poets live as they write.
When I am dead in the dark I am dark and dead,
but the first new word spells the end of that night.

The long silence is the pause between breaths,
the wait in the grave, then the call to rise.
And, like resurrection, newly-taken air is me made new,
seeing again with fresh-made eyes.

I am writing, so living.
It pulses like the beat.
This is the heart of me,
this is my call.
To hear and to learn is as good as to eat.

Your Spirit

When I can't hear you, O Lord,
Your Spirit finds a way to shout.

When I can't pray, O Lord,
Your Spirit helps me to say what I need to say.

When I can't say, O Lord,
Your Spirit helps me to feel what I need to feel.

When I can't feel, O Lord,
Your Spirit feels for me.

When I'm at rock bottom, O Lord,
Your Spirit shows me you, here beside me,
there leading me forward.

When I'm well, O Lord, and find it easy to hear
and pray and say and feel,
I need your Spirit just as much.

Epilogue

My adolescence, that period of turmoil and change for us all, was for me filled with faith (new commitment to Christ, beginnings of vocation to the priesthood and joy in worship) and anxiety (at boarding school, a hard environment, separated from my family and struggling with sexual awakening).

Anxiety is a repressed backdrop to my life still. When Depression gets a grip on me, usually each year, Anxiety adds to its crippling hold on me and can last for months.

I have long—over fifty years—experience of this, and know that faith (devotional life, ministry, public worship) cannot by itself break the hold of this illness. And that maybe medical help (drugs, talking therapies, and so on) only contains but does not cure it. It runs its course and I emerge again.

If you too suffer in this sort of way, what is really important is to acknowledge it, to be aware of what sorts of things can bring it on and always to be realistic without being fatalistic.

It is not inevitable that you will become ill. But recognise the triggers. For me it might be the yearly "Dying of the Light" or plain exhaustion, disappointment or getting thoroughly stressed out.

Develop strategies to use against these pressures and always be kind to yourself. When you are well, prepare for and guard against the next onset of illness. It may happen but it is not inevitable. Never be fatalistic. Prepare to stay well instead.

I welcome the opportunity to have said all this. And the community of the isolated and imprisoned, all of us Depressives, are dear and loved people. If you pray, pray for yourself, for me and us all. Light is stronger than darkness and a new day always dawns.

David

A Depression and Anxiety sufferer, but more than this, a loved child of God.

Resources for further help

It's not the purpose of this book to comment or advise on medical issues and help. Here are a few other suggestions.

There are many **Books** on the market on our subject by Christian authors on most of the main Christian publishing lists. You may want to look for ones from your own particular culture and background, though there is value in the cross-grained experience of reading where you do not usually look.

I particularly recommend *From Over the Edge: A Christian's guide to surviving Breakdown & Depression* by Jon Grogan (Sacristy Press, 2016). It is available from www.sacristy.co.uk.

There are also audio, even video **programs** available to buy and download. Be discerning! Not all out there is of the same quality or of most help to you.

Self-help groups and magazines are available and a browser search will help.

Personal contacts. There may be family members, trusted, good friends, Priests and Ministers in whom you can confide and share your story. Do seek them out. They will want to share your load as far as they can.

Sometimes **prayer and worship** can be difficult for a depressed Christian in illness. Please don't feel this is at all wrong. Others can pray for you, with you (if this is what you wish), and instead of you. Your task in the Church at the time is to seek to get well. The others will do their own tasks.

And at all times, seek to remember the **Presence of Christ**, crucified, risen, ascended, interceding for you, always with you.